The Power of Being You. Copyright © 2025 by Amanda Peng

ISBN: 978-91-89876-21-7

All Rights Reserved. No part of this work may be reproduced, incorporated into a computer system, or transmitted in any form or by any means (electronic, mechanical, photocopying, recording or otherwise) without the prior written permission of the copyright holders. Infringement of such rights may constitute an intellectual property crime.

THE POWER OF BEING YOU

Oubaitori

Amanda Peng

CONTENTS

Introduction The Gift of Your Own Bloom	6
I - The Art of Blooming at Your Own Pace	10
II - The Unseen Roots of Growth	16
III - Inner Dialogue – The Voice That Shapes Your Oubaitori Journey	22
IV - Gratitude – The Key to a Fulfilling Life	26
V - Embrace the Beauty of Your Uniqueness	30
VI - The Art of Flourishing – Embracing Your Unique Growth	35
VII - The Joy of Celebration – Honoring Your Journey	41
VIII - Design Your Own Path	47
IX - Flourishing in Community	52
X - The Impact of Blooming at Your Own Pace	57
XI - The Silent Forest – Finding Strength in Stillness	62
XII - Weathering the Storm – Cultivating Resilience Through Oubaitori	68
XIII - Growing Through the Storm – Oubaitori in Times of Crisis	74
XIV - Cultivating Professional Success Through Oubaitori	79

XV - Flourishing in Relationships Through Oubaitori   84

XVI - Cultivating Health Through Oubaitori   89

Epilogue - The Symphony of Your Own Bloom   94

Final Chapter - Your Journey Begins: A Practical Guide to
Embracing Oubaitori   97

Introduction
The Gift of Your Own Bloom

On a crisp spring morning, I found myself standing in a remote Japanese garden, tucked away in the rolling hills outside Kyoto. The air was still, yet alive with the quiet energy of nature. Before me stood four trees: a cherry, a plum, a peach, and an apricot. The cherry was in full bloom, its pink blossoms vibrant against the morning light. The plum tree had just begun to bud, its delicate shoots hinting at the life to come. The peach tree stood bare, its branches stretching skyward in quiet anticipation. Meanwhile, the apricot carried the remnants of its earlier bloom, petals scattered like whispers across the ground. Each tree told its own story, unfolding in its own time.

The gardener, an elderly man with hands worn by decades of care, noticed my gaze. "They bloom when it's their time," he said, his voice soft but resolute. "No tree is rushing to be like the other. They just are. And that is their strength."

I stood there, struck by the profound simplicity of his words. How often in life do we rush to match the pace of others, to measure ourselves against timelines not our own? We live in a world that glorifies comparison and urgency, yet here was nature's quiet reminder: every bloom has its season, and every season has its purpose.
This moment stayed with me, planting a seed in my mind. I realized how much of my own life had

been shaped by the pressures to conform, to compare, to keep up. And I wondered—what would it feel like to live differently? To embrace my own rhythm, my own bloom?

What If You Are Enough?

Imagine a life where you wake up without the weight of comparison on your shoulders. A life where your worth isn't tied to how fast you achieve, how perfectly you perform, or how seamlessly you fit into societal molds. What if you could let go of the notion that you're falling behind, and instead trust that you are exactly where you're meant to be?

This is the essence of **Oubaitori**—a Japanese philosophy that teaches us to honor our unique growth. The word itself comes from the kanji characters representing the four trees I saw that morning: cherry, plum, peach, and apricot. Each blooms in its own time, each is beautiful in its own way, and none is diminished by the other.

Oubaitori is not about rejecting ambition or abandoning goals. It's about aligning your journey with your own nature, rather than someone else's expectations. It's about recognizing that your path, no matter how unconventional or nonlinear, is valid and valuable.

Why This Book, and Why Now?

We live in an era of relentless comparison. Social media feeds us curated highlights of other people's lives, making us question our own choices. The workplace often feels like a race, with success measured by rigid metrics and arbitrary timelines. Even in our personal lives, we struggle with the subtle but pervasive pressure to "keep up."

But what if the solution isn't to keep up, but to slow down? To step back and ask: What do I truly value? What brings me joy? What does success mean to me — not to others, but to me?

This book is an invitation to explore those questions. Through the lens of Oubaitori, we'll journey together through the key aspects of life — self-discovery, relationships, work, health, and community. You'll learn how to embrace your individuality, celebrate your unique strengths, and create a life that feels authentic and fulfilling.

A Conversation Between Us

Think of this book not as a lecture, but as a conversation — a dialogue between you and me. My goal isn't to tell you how to live your life, but to offer stories, insights, and tools that might help you live it more fully. Together, we'll explore what it means to honor your own pace, to find beauty in your imperfections, and to trust the timing of your journey.

I won't pretend that this path is easy. It requires courage to step away from comparison, to silence the voices of doubt and judgment, and to embrace the uncertainty of your own rhythm. But I promise you this: the reward is worth it. When you live in alignment with who you truly are, life becomes richer, deeper, and more meaningful.

Your Journey Begins Here

As you turn the pages of this book, I invite you to approach it with an open heart and a spirit of curiosity. Let the ideas take root within you. Reflect on them, challenge them, and make them your own.

The cherry tree doesn't envy the plum. The peach doesn't strive to be the apricot. Each blooms when it's ready, in its own way, creating a symphony of diversity and beauty.

So too can you.

Welcome to the journey of Oubaitori. Let's begin.

I
The Art of Blooming at Your Own Pace

The Cherry Tree That Refused to Bloom

It was a chilly spring morning in the quiet Japanese countryside. The village was alive with the soft hum of anticipation, as locals and travelers alike prepared for the hanami season. Blankets were spread beneath rows of cherry trees, and children ran in circles, laughing as their parents unpacked bento boxes. But amidst the anticipation of cherry blossoms painting the sky pink, one tree stood bare.

Its branches stretched out like skeletal fingers, stark against the blue sky. Whispered judgments rippled through the crowd: "Maybe it's too old", "Or too weak", "Poor tree".

Nearby, an elderly man with a serene smile listened without reacting. He quietly approached the bare tree, his steps deliberate, his gaze tender. Turning to the crowd, he spoke, his voice calm but commanding: "This tree isn't late. It's waiting. Its moment will come. And when it blooms, it will show us a beauty we've never seen before."

The doubters laughed nervously, dismissing the old man's words. But two weeks later, when most cherry blossoms had already begun to fall, this lone tree erupted into an explosion of pink. Its flowers were larger, more radiant, and more fragrant than any other tree in the grove.

Silence replaced the whispers, and awe replaced doubt.

The tree became a symbol for the village—a reminder that each of us blooms in our own time.

This story isn't just about a cherry tree. It's about you. It's about me. It's about every person who's ever felt "too late" or "not enough." In a world that pushes us to keep up with others, the Japanese philosophy of **Oubaitori**—a lesson written in the language of nature—offers us a liberating truth: you don't have to follow anyone else's timeline.

Understanding Oubaitori

Oubaitori (桜梅桃李) is more than a word. It's a profound way of understanding the human experience. The term combines four kanji characters, each representing a tree that blooms in its own season:

- **Sakura (桜):** The cherry tree, revered for its fleeting, ethereal beauty. Its blossoms symbolize the fragility and impermanence of life.
- **Ume (梅):** The plum tree, which blooms early, defying winter's harshness. It's a symbol of resilience and quiet strength.
- **Momo (桃):** The peach tree, celebrated for its lush blossoms and sweet fruits, heralding the arrival of spring.
- **Uri (李):** The apricot tree, the last to bloom, offering understated flowers but rich, golden fruits that nourish long after spring has passed.

These trees often grow side by side, but they don't compete. They don't rush or envy one another.

Each blooms in its own season, offering unique beauty and purpose to the landscape.

Imagine applying this principle to your own life. What if you could stop comparing yourself to others? What if you could honor your own rhythm, trusting that your time will come?

Why Comparisons Are So Toxic

We live in an age of relentless comparison. Social media platforms bombard us with polished snapshots of other people's lives: the promotion, the dream wedding, the perfect vacation. Each image whispers the same insidious question: "Why aren't you there yet?"

But here's the truth: **comparison is a thief.** It steals your joy, your peace, and your ability to appreciate your own progress.

Psychological studies reveal just how damaging this habit can be. A groundbreaking 2020 study published in the *Journal of Behavioral Science* found that people who frequently compared themselves to others were over 40% more likely to report feelings of anxiety and depression. The act of comparison activates the brain's reward system, but instead of satisfaction, it creates an endless loop of dissatisfaction.

Consider the story of Emi, a young woman from Osaka. For years, Emi felt trapped in the shadow of her older sister, Yuki. While Yuki climbed the corporate ladder, earning accolades and promotions, Emi struggled to find her path. "Every family dinner was a reminder of what I wasn't," Emi confessed. "I couldn't see past her success to appreciate my own journey."

Everything changed when Emi stumbled upon a poetry workshop. Writing awakened something inside her—a voice uniquely her own. Over time, her words gained recognition, and she became a published poet. "When I stopped looking at Yuki's path," Emi reflected, "I finally saw my own."

Seizing the Power of Your Unique Bloom

Here's a radical thought: what if you celebrated your timing instead of resenting it? Oubaitori teaches us that no bloom is less valuable for arriving later or earlier. Just as the ume tree's resilience inspires us during winter and the sakura's beauty enchants us in spring, each stage of your journey holds its own magic.

In 2015, a fascinating study from Stanford University revealed that people who focused on self-comparison—tracking their growth relative to their past selves—were significantly happier and more productive than those who compared themselves to peers. The key isn't to eliminate ambition but to direct it inward.

Let's return to the trees for a moment. The sakura doesn't try to bloom in winter; the ume doesn't strive to be a peach. Each tree stands rooted in its essence, knowing its role in the grand tapestry of life.

Lessons You Can Apply Today

1. Track Your Progress, Not Others' Paths:

Begin keeping a "growth journal." Instead of fixating on external achievements, jot down small victories: a challenge you overcame, a skill you improved, or a lesson you learned.

2. **Ask the Right Questions:**

Replace "Why am I not where they are?" with "What can I learn from my journey so far?" and "What unique gifts do I bring to the world?"

3. **Practice Gratitude Daily:**

Create a gratitude ritual. Each evening, write down three things you're grateful for—not grand achievements, but quiet moments that remind you of your progress.

4. **Limit Social Media:**

Take a break from platforms that fuel unhealthy comparisons. Replace scrolling with activities that nurture you, like reading, walking, or journaling.

5. **Celebrate Micro-Wins:**

Big milestones don't happen overnight. Honor the small steps—finishing a book, cooking a new recipe, reaching out to a friend. These moments are the petals of your bloom.

Conclusion: A New Way to See Yourself

Imagine standing in a vast garden. Around you, cherry trees, plum trees, peach trees, and apricot trees bloom at different times. Some are already bearing fruit; others are still budding. Each adds to the beauty of the scene in its own way.

Now imagine that you're one of those trees. Your branches may not yet be full of blossoms, and that's okay. Your time will come. When it does, your bloom will be like no other—a reflection of your unique journey, struggles, and triumphs.

Oubaitori isn't just a philosophy; it's a way of living. It's an invitation to trust yourself, to honor your timing, and to celebrate your growth—no matter where you are in your journey.

So take a deep breath. Stop measuring yourself against the timeline of others. You are blooming exactly as you're meant to.

And when you finally see your blossoms, you'll know they were worth the wait.

II
The Unseen Roots of Growth

The Bamboo's Secret

In a dense forest in Kyushu, Japan, a farmer planted a grove of bamboo. He watered the soil diligently every day, even when nothing seemed to happen. For months, the ground remained bare. Neighbors began to chuckle behind his back, calling him foolish. But the farmer kept at it, tending to the invisible.

Then, in the fifth year, something extraordinary occurred. The bamboo, dormant for so long, began to grow. And not just a little—some stalks shot up as much as three feet in a single day. Within weeks, the grove transformed into a towering forest.

The secret? Those five years of "nothing" were not wasted. During that time, the bamboo had been developing an intricate root system underground, creating a foundation strong enough to support its rapid ascent.

The lesson is simple yet profound: **growth isn't always visible.** Just like bamboo, our most important development often happens beneath the surface, in places no one can see. Oubaitori reminds us that this hidden work is not only valid but vital. Before we can bloom, we must root ourselves deeply.

What Lies Beneath the Surface

The modern world celebrates results: promotions, accolades, degrees, followers. But the groundwork—the quiet, unseen effort that makes these achievements possible—often goes unrecognized. This disconnect creates frustration and impatience. We look at others' successes and wonder, "Why not me?" without considering the invisible roots they've nurtured to get there.

Take, for example, the late bloomers who changed the world. Vincent van Gogh sold only one painting in his lifetime. Colonel Harland Sanders founded KFC at age 65. Nobel laureate Toni Morrison published her first novel at 39, after years of working as an editor and raising children. Their early struggles didn't define them because they spent those years planting their roots: honing their skills, building resilience, and learning lessons that would fuel their eventual success.

The Science of Hidden Growth

Modern neuroscience provides fascinating insights into the concept of unseen growth. The brain is like a bamboo forest, requiring time to build its networks before it can achieve peak performance.

A 2016 study at Harvard University revealed that deep practice—repeatedly engaging in challenging tasks without immediate visible improvement—creates stronger neural connections. These connections, much like the bamboo's roots, prepare the mind for breakthroughs.

For example, think of a student struggling with a foreign language. The early stages feel futile, with slow progress and constant mistakes. But under the surface, the brain is rewiring itself. One day, seemingly out of nowhere, fluency clicks. This "overnight success" is anything but—it's the result of months or years of unseen growth.

Stories That Will Change How You See Progress

The Tale of Two Gardens

Imagine two gardens side by side. The first gardener prioritizes quick results, planting fast-growing flowers that bloom within weeks. The second gardener plants an oak tree. For years, the first garden looks vibrant, while the second appears barren.

But as the seasons pass, the oak begins to grow, its branches spreading wide, its roots stretching deep. The flowers, meanwhile, have withered. Decades later, the oak stands as a monument to endurance, shading generations and weathering storms.

This isn't just a metaphor. The oak tree represents lasting growth—built slowly, with intention and care. The flowers? They're the short-lived rewards that fade as quickly as they appear.

The Chess Prodigy Who Waited

Judit Polgár, one of the greatest chess players in history, offers another remarkable example. Her parents began teaching her chess at the age of four, but she didn't play in her first tournament until much later. Instead of rushing to compete, she spent years studying classic matches, analyzing mistakes, and developing her strategy.

When she finally entered the competitive arena, she stunned the chess world. Many called her success "effortless," not realizing it was built on years of quiet preparation.

Leaning Into the Quiet Seasons of Life

There are times when life feels stagnant, as if nothing is happening despite your efforts. These "quiet seasons" are often the most crucial. They're the periods when you're laying the foundation for the next chapter of your life.

The Japanese concept of *ma* — the pause or space between actions — aligns beautifully with Oubaitori. *Ma* teaches us to embrace stillness, recognizing that what feels like a lull is often the prelude to transformation.

For instance, think of artists. Before the masterpiece, there are countless drafts and discarded attempts. Before the symphony, there are hours of silence spent composing notes. What looks like stagnation is actually incubation.

Lessons You Can Apply Today

1. **Respect the Invisible Work:**

Stop dismissing your quiet efforts as "wasted time." Every late night studying, every practice session, every moment of self-reflection is part of your root system.

2. **Journal the Process:**

Keep a journal not just for milestones but for the in-between moments. Write about what you're learning, how you're growing, and where you're struggling. This will help you see progress even when it feels invisible.

3. **Create a Long-Term Vision:**

Just like the bamboo farmer, focus on the long game. Set goals that prioritize sustainable growth over quick wins. Ask yourself, "What roots do I need to plant today for tomorrow's success?"

4. Surround Yourself with Patience:

Spend time with people who value the process, not just the results. These individuals will remind you that slow growth is still growth.

5. Find Joy in the Quiet:

Embrace activities that nourish your spirit—reading, meditating, walking in nature. These moments of stillness are fertile ground for inspiration.

Conclusion: Trust the Roots

The bamboo doesn't question its five years of dormancy. It doesn't rush itself or compare its growth to the flowers around it. It simply trusts the process.

Imagine if you could do the same. What if you stopped rushing, comparing, or doubting your journey? What if you trusted that every effort, no matter how small or unseen, was contributing to your future?

Take a moment now to reflect on your own "root system." Where are you quietly growing? What unseen strengths are you cultivating?

As you move forward, remember this: growth isn't always visible, but that doesn't make it any less real. When your time comes to rise, you'll do so with the strength of roots that run deep—and that will make all the difference.

Let the world rush. You are building something enduring. Something beautiful. Something uniquely yours.

III

Inner Dialogue – The Voice That Shapes Your Oubaitori Journey

The Seeds of Your Story

Imagine walking through a serene Japanese garden. Each tree—plum, cherry, peach, and apricot—stands apart, growing at its own rhythm. The plum tree blooms early, its vibrant flowers defying the cold. The cherry tree waits patiently for the warmth of spring. Each tree thrives in its unique timing, unbothered by the pace of others.

Now consider this: how often does your inner dialogue—your constant mental chatter—compare you to someone else's "season"? How often does it tell you that you're too late, too slow, or not enough?

The philosophy of Oubaitori teaches us to honor our individuality, yet it begins with the voice inside us. The narrative you tell yourself shapes how you experience your journey. This chapter explores the art of transforming your inner dialogue to support, rather than hinder, your personal growth.

The Dialogue That Defines Growth

In Oubaitori, each tree represents a different rhythm of growth, but the gardener's care is consistent. Think of your inner dialogue as the gardener of your mind. Does it nurture you with kindness, or does it harshly prune every perceived flaw?

Psychologists have identified that our inner voice plays a critical role in how we navigate life. Negative self-talk, often rooted in comparison, stunts growth by reinforcing feelings of inadequacy. Meanwhile, a compassionate inner dialogue encourages resilience and creativity.

Research on *self-compassion* by Dr. Kristin Neff reveals that speaking kindly to oneself isn't indulgent—it's transformative. Self-compassion helps us recover from setbacks, embrace imperfections, and persist in the face of challenges.

In the context of Oubaitori, this means silencing the inner critic that says, "You should be blooming like them," and replacing it with a voice that whispers, "You're growing beautifully at your own pace."

The Tale of the Misfit Bonsai

In Kyoto, there is a bonsai tree that doesn't follow the traditional standards of perfection. Its trunk is crooked, its branches asymmetrical, and its growth defies the meticulous rules of bonsai cultivation. Initially, it was considered a "failure." Yet over time, the tree became celebrated for its unique form, symbolizing the beauty of imperfection.

The gardener who cared for it didn't try to force it into a standard mold. Instead, he listened to what the tree needed, adapting his techniques to its natural tendencies.

Your inner dialogue can either act as the rigid bonsai master, trying to mold you into someone else's ideal, or as the compassionate gardener, guiding you toward your own authentic growth. The choice is yours.

Practical Lessons: Cultivating a Supportive Inner Dialogue

1. **The Oubaitori Reflexion Exercise**

Every morning, look in the mirror and affirm your own growth by stating:

- "I honor my own pace of growth."
- "I embrace my unique journey."
- "I bloom in my own time."

> These affirmations, grounded in the philosophy of Oubaitori, help rewire your inner dialogue to align with self-acceptance.

2. **Rewrite the Narrative**

When a self-critical thought arises, pause and write it down. Then, reframe it in a way that honors your individuality. For instance:

> **Critical thought**: "I'm not as successful as my peers."
> **Reframed thought**: "My growth is unique, and my time to bloom will come."

3. **The Growth Journal**

Dedicate a section of your journal to reflecting on personal progress. Instead of focusing on outcomes, document small wins, moments of courage, or lessons learned. This helps shift your focus from comparison to self-recognition.

4. Practice the "Tree Talk"

Choose a quiet moment to imagine speaking to your inner self as if it were one of the trees in Oubaitori. What would you say to nurture its growth? How would you encourage its natural rhythm?

Conclusion: Becoming the Gardener of Your Mind

Oubaitori teaches us that every tree has its season, yet the strength of the roots determines the beauty of the bloom. Your inner dialogue is like those roots — it anchors you, nourishes you, and determines how you face life's challenges.

When you choose compassion over criticism, you become the master gardener of your mind, cultivating a space where your unique growth can flourish. Remember: the trees don't compare themselves, and neither should you.

As you continue your Oubaitori journey, let your inner dialogue reflect the beauty of your individuality. What story will you tell yourself today? Will it be one of limitation, or one of boundless potential?

The voice inside you is the narrator of your life. Make it a voice worth listening to.

IV

Gratitude – The Key to a Fulfilling Life

A Cup of Tea and a World of Gratitude

In a small teahouse nestled in the hills of Kyoto, a tea master begins his daily ritual. Every movement—pouring the water, whisking the matcha, serving the bowl—is deliberate, almost reverent. Before taking his first sip, he pauses. Bowing his head slightly, he whispers a simple phrase: *"Arigatou gozaimasu."* Thank you.

He's not thanking someone else. He's thanking the tea itself—the leaves that grew under the sun, the water that traveled from the mountains, the cup that holds this moment together.

Gratitude is woven into Japanese culture, not as a grand gesture, but as an everyday practice. This is the essence of Oubaitori: appreciating the beauty of your unique path while honoring the forces that sustain you along the way. Gratitude doesn't just enrich your life; it transforms it.

Gratitude and the Oubaitori Philosophy

Gratitude is the bridge between what you have and the joy you seek. In the philosophy of Oubaitori, gratitude helps us honor our individuality while recognizing the interconnectedness of life.

Think of the plum, cherry, peach, and apricot trees. Each blooms in its own season, yet each is sustained by the same soil, sun, and rain. Gratitude allows us to acknowledge these unseen forces that support our growth.

Modern science supports what ancient wisdom has long known: practicing gratitude rewires the brain. Studies from institutions like Harvard and Berkeley reveal that people who regularly express gratitude experience increased happiness, reduced stress, and stronger relationships. Gratitude shifts your focus from scarcity to abundance, from comparison to contentment.

In Oubaitori, gratitude is more than a fleeting emotion—it's a practice, a way of seeing and honoring the journey.

The Legend of the Stonecutter

There is a Japanese tale of a stonecutter who spent his days carving rocks. Dissatisfied with his life, he wished to be as powerful as the sun. Magically, his wish was granted.

But as the sun, he realized he could be blocked by clouds. He wished to be the clouds. Then, as clouds, he saw that mountains could stand taller. He wished to be the mountain. Eventually, he realized the stonecutter, with his hammer and chisel, could shape the mountain itself.

With a newfound sense of gratitude, he returned to his original form, embracing his life as a stonecutter. His perspective had changed. What he once saw as mundane, he now saw as meaningful.

This story reminds us that gratitude isn't about waiting for external changes—it's about shifting how we see what's already within us and around us.

Practical Lessons: Cultivating Gratitude in Your Daily Life

1.The "Three Blossoms" Practice

Every evening, write down three things you are grateful for—one from your past, one from your present, and one for your future. For example:

- Past: "I'm grateful for the teacher who encouraged me when I doubted myself."
- Present: "I'm grateful for the warm meal I had today."
- Future: "I'm grateful for the opportunities I know are coming."

This practice helps you see your life as a continuous bloom, with each phase offering its own gifts.

2. Gratitude Walks

Go for a walk and actively notice the details around you. The crunch of leaves under your feet. The sound of birdsong. The way the sunlight filters through the trees. Whisper a quiet *thank you* for each small wonder you observe.

3. The Gratitude Letter

Write a letter to someone who has shaped your journey—a mentor, a friend, a family member. You don't even have to send it. The act of writing it down solidifies your connection to the people who have supported your growth.

4. Morning Gratitude Ritual

Begin your day with a moment of gratitude. Before reaching for your phone or starting your tasks, take a deep breath and say aloud:

- "Thank you for another day to grow."
- "Thank you for the challenges that make me stronger."

Conclusion: Gratitude as the Foundation of Oubaitori

Gratitude is the soil in which your growth takes root. Without it, even the most vibrant blooms will struggle to thrive. With it, even the smallest sprout feels like a miracle.

As you walk the path of Oubaitori, remember to pause and give thanks—not just for the moments of success, but for the challenges, the lessons, and the quiet beauty of your unique journey.

When you practice gratitude, you align yourself with the rhythms of life, just as the plum, cherry, peach, and apricot trees honor their own seasons.

Take a moment now to reflect: What are you grateful for in this very moment? Hold that thought close. Let it anchor you, nourish you, and remind you of the extraordinary gift of being alive.

Gratitude doesn't just change your perspective—it changes your life.

V
Embrace the Beauty of Your Uniqueness

The Story of the Misfit Clay Pot

In a quiet corner of a bustling Kyoto pottery market, there was a shop known for its "imperfect" pieces. Among the shelves, a clay pot stood out. Its surface was uneven, its shape slightly lopsided. Next to sleek, symmetrical vases, this pot seemed misplaced.

One day, a curious customer asked the shopkeeper why the pot was even for sale. The shopkeeper smiled and poured water into the pot. As the water flowed out, the uneven surface caught the light, casting patterns of shimmering ripples on the walls.

"This pot tells a story," the shopkeeper said. "Its beauty lies in what others call flaws. No other pot in the world creates these patterns of light."

This clay pot, with its unique imperfections, mirrors the essence of Oubaitori: there is beauty in what makes us different. The world doesn't need replicas; it needs your authentic light.

The Power of Being Unrepeatable

The Japanese concept of *wabi-sabi* — the art of embracing imperfection — teaches us to value the unique beauty of things that are incomplete or unconventional. This principle aligns with

Oubaitori, where individuality is celebrated rather than suppressed.

But society often pushes us in the opposite direction. From a young age, we are taught to measure ourselves against standardized benchmarks: grades in school, career milestones, physical appearances. This constant comparison chips away at our confidence, convincing us that we need to change, conform, or improve to be "enough."

What if the very things we are trying to erase are the key to our greatness? Research from the University of California shows that self-acceptance is a cornerstone of lasting happiness. People who embrace their quirks and differences experience deeper satisfaction and stronger relationships.

Just like the cherry, plum, peach, and apricot trees of Oubaitori, you were never meant to grow in the same way as anyone else. Your value isn't in how you compare but in how you stand apart.

The Strength of the Snowflake

Snowflakes are often used as a metaphor for individuality. Each one is unique, a product of countless variables in its formation. But snowflakes are also fragile—prone to melting at the slightest touch.

Yet, when snowflakes gather, they form blankets of snow that transform landscapes. They create avalanches powerful enough to reshape mountains.

This duality of fragility and strength reflects the human experience. Your uniqueness might feel like a vulnerability, but when embraced, it becomes a source of incredible power.

One example is Temple Grandin, a scientist with autism who revolutionized the livestock industry. Grandin's condition, once considered a limitation, allowed her to see patterns and solutions others couldn't. By embracing her unique perspective, she reshaped an entire field.

Your individuality is an untapped reservoir of potential.

Practical Lessons: Uncovering Your Unique Beauty

1. **The Mirror Exercise**

Stand in front of a mirror and look at yourself, not with judgment but with curiosity. Instead of focusing on perceived flaws, ask yourself:

- What makes me *me*?
- What stories do my scars, features, and expressions tell?
- What have these elements of myself allowed me to experience?

Practice seeing yourself as an evolving masterpiece, not a work-in-progress needing correction.

2. **Write Your Unique Story**

Take a moment to reflect on the traits or experiences that set you apart. Write them down in a journal, focusing on how each has contributed to your growth. For example:

- "I am empathetic because I've faced struggles."
- "I think differently, which allows me to solve problems creatively."

This exercise helps you reframe your differences as strengths.

3. Celebrate an Unconventional Strength

Think about a trait that society might label as a weakness. How has this trait served you? For instance:

- If you're introverted, perhaps it's given you the ability to listen deeply and form meaningful connections.
- If you're outspoken, perhaps it's allowed you to advocate for others.

Write a letter of gratitude to this trait, thanking it for shaping your journey.

4. Create Your Uniqueness Portfolio

Compile a list of your unique qualities, skills, and passions. Use this as a personal reminder whenever you feel tempted to compare yourself to others. For example:

- "I have a deep love for music that brings people together."
- "My sense of humor lightens difficult situations."

This portfolio is a testament to the beauty of your individuality.

Conclusion: Blooming as You Are

The world doesn't need another cherry tree; it needs you, in all your complexity and brilliance. Your journey, like the clay pot in the Kyoto shop, isn't about perfection—it's about the patterns of light you cast.

Embracing your uniqueness is an act of courage in a world that often demands conformity. But remember: no one else has lived your story, faced your challenges, or dreamed your dreams.

As you walk the path of Oubaitori, resist the urge to compare your bloom to someone else's. Instead, focus on nurturing the soil of your individuality. Each twist in your journey, each "flaw" you see in yourself, contributes to the radiant mosaic of your life.

Take a deep breath and whisper to yourself:

- "I am enough, exactly as I am."
- "I am blooming at my own pace, in my own way."

You are a masterpiece in progress, and the world is brighter because of your light. Embrace it fully.

VI

The Art of Flourishing – Embracing Your Unique Growth

A Garden of Infinite Possibilities

Imagine a vast and vibrant garden, each plant growing in its own time, its own way. Some bloom quickly, their flowers bright and bold, while others take years to unfold, revealing a deeper, quieter beauty. Now picture a gardener, walking through this space, marveling at the diversity—not comparing one plant to another, but appreciating the distinct character of each.

This is the essence of flourishing: not striving to mimic others, but thriving in your own way. Yet, in a world obsessed with comparison, how can we shift our focus from what others are achieving to the beauty of our unique growth?

This chapter is a call to action, inviting you to step into your metaphorical garden and tend to the life that is uniquely yours. By understanding what flourishing means for you—and only you—you can transform your journey into one of profound fulfillment.

The Anatomy of Flourishing

Flourishing is often mistaken for success in the conventional sense—achieving status, wealth, or recognition. But true flourishing is far richer and more nuanced. It's about living in alignment with your values, cultivating inner joy, and nurturing your potential in ways that feel authentic.

Psychologist Martin Seligman, a pioneer in the field of positive psychology, describes flourishing as having five core elements, often referred to as the PERMA model:

- **Positive Emotion:** Experiencing joy, gratitude, and contentment.
- **Engagement:** Being deeply involved in activities that challenge and inspire you.
- **Relationships:** Building meaningful connections with others.
- **Meaning:** Pursuing a sense of purpose that transcends the self.
- **Accomplishment:** Achieving goals that matter to you personally.

Let's take this framework and layer it with the philosophy of Oubaitori. Flourishing doesn't happen in comparison to others — it unfolds when you honor your individual rhythm, much like the cherry blossom, plum, peach, and apricot trees that bloom at their own time and in their own way.

When Growth is Invisible

The Hidden Growth Paradox

There's a common tendency to judge growth by what is immediately visible. Consider the story of a sculptor working on a large marble block. At first, all that is seen is the rough, unpolished stone, with seemingly little progress. Days and weeks pass, and yet, the form within the stone is still hidden beneath layers of dust and debris. But little by little, the sculptor chips away, refining the shape, until one day, the masterpiece emerges, revealing the beauty that was always there.

How often do we dismiss our own development because the results aren't immediately apparent? Like the sculptor with their marble, the most meaningful progress often occurs beneath the surface, in the quiet, uncelebrated work of laying a strong foundation. The key is to trust the process and understand that transformation is happening, even when it's invisible to the outside world.

The Story of Yayoi Kusama

Japanese artist Yayoi Kusama, now celebrated worldwide for her avant-garde work, spent decades in obscurity. Her art, marked by obsessive patterns and vibrant colors, was unlike anything else at the time. She faced rejection, ridicule, and even a battle with mental illness. Yet, she continued to create — not for fame, but because it was her authentic expression. Today, her works are iconic, and her journey reminds us that flourishing is not about instant recognition but about staying true to our unique vision.

The Common Pitfall: Blooming Too Soon

In the rush to achieve, many of us try to force growth prematurely, seeking shortcuts or external validation. But just as forcing a flower to bloom can weaken its stem, rushing your own development can leave you vulnerable to burnout and dissatisfaction.

Consider the phenomenon of "instant success". Social media often amplifies stories of people who seem to achieve greatness overnight. What these narratives rarely reveal are the years of unseen effort, failures, and perseverance. When we compare our progress to these curated highlights, we risk undervaluing our own journey.

Practical Lessons for Your Unique Flourishing

Lesson 1: Define Your Own Bloom

Flourishing begins with clarity. What does a meaningful, fulfilling life look like for you?

- **Exercise:** Create a "Flourishing Vision Board." Collect images, words, and symbols that resonate with your idea of a flourishing life. This could include personal goals, values, or simply feelings you want to cultivate. Display it somewhere visible as a daily reminder.

Lesson 2: Honor Your Seasons

Just as plants have seasons of growth, rest, and renewal, so do we. Recognizing your current season can help you set realistic expectations and avoid unnecessary frustration.

- **Exercise:** Reflect on your life right now. Are you in a season of planting (laying foundations), blooming (active growth), or resting (recharging your energy)? Adjust your goals and self-expectations accordingly.

Lesson 3: Nurture, Don't Neglect

Growth requires consistent care, but not force. Focus on creating the right conditions for your personal flourishing—mentally, emotionally, and physically.

- **Exercise:** Identify one area of your life that feels

neglected. It could be your health, a creative passion, or a relationship. Dedicate 15 minutes a day to nurturing this area, whether that means taking a walk, writing a poem, or calling a loved one.

Lesson 4: Release Comparisons

Comparing your growth to others is like measuring an oak tree by the standards of a rose. Both are beautiful, but their paths are entirely different.

- **Exercise:** Start a "Comparison Detox." For one week, consciously avoid comparing yourself to others in one specific area (e.g., career, appearance, relationships). Instead, celebrate one personal accomplishment or quality each day.

The Beauty of Interdependence

While flourishing is deeply personal, it doesn't happen in isolation. Just as the trees in a forest share resources through underground root systems, we thrive when we connect with others in meaningful ways.

Consider the Japanese concept of *kyosei* (共生), which means "living together in harmony". It emphasizes mutual support and cooperation, reminding us that flourishing doesn't mean going it alone. Building a community that nurtures your growth—and contributing to the growth of others—creates a powerful cycle of resilience and inspiration.

Conclusion: Becoming the Gardener of Your Life

Flourishing is not a destination; it's a practice. It's the way you tend to your life, day by day, with care and intention. Like the gardener in the opening image, you have the power to cultivate a space where your unique growth can unfold.

Take a moment to imagine yourself in that garden. What does it look like? What are you nurturing? And what steps can you take today to ensure your roots grow strong and your branches reach toward the light?

In the next chapter, we'll delve into the transformative power of celebration—not just for the milestones you achieve, but for the journey itself. Because every step forward, every act of care, is a bloom worth honoring.

VII

The Joy of Celebration – Honoring Your Journey

A Toast to the Small Wins

It's a crisp evening in Kyoto, and the streets are alive with the gentle hum of conversation and laughter. Families and friends gather beneath the cherry blossoms, their pink petals illuminated by lanterns that sway in the cool breeze. This is *hanami* — the Japanese tradition of celebrating the fleeting beauty of flowers. For centuries, this ritual has invited people to pause, reflect, and rejoice in the transient splendor of life.

What if we adopted this mindset, not just for cherry blossoms, but for our own lives? What if we learned to honor each step of our journey, no matter how small, with the same reverence and joy?

This chapter explores the art of celebration as a transformative practice, a way to fuel your growth, deepen your appreciation for life, and build resilience. We are going to notice — and celebrate — the beauty of the process itself.

The Science of Celebration: Fuel for Flourishing

Celebration isn't just a feel-good moment; it's a powerful psychological tool. Studies in neuroscience reveal that when we celebrate, our brain releases dopamine — a neurotransmitter associated with pleasure and motivation. This surge of dopamine not only makes us feel good in the moment but also reinforces the behavior we're celebrating, making us more likely to repeat it.

In other words, celebration is a self-reinforcing cycle of positivity. When you take time to acknowledge your progress, you're creating an internal feedback loop that fuels your motivation and helps you stay the course.

Yet many of us are quick to dismiss our achievements. We focus on what's left to do rather than what we've already done, denying ourselves the joy of the moment. By learning to pause and celebrate, we reclaim a vital source of energy and inspiration.

Lessons from Unexpected Celebrations

The Marathoner's Mile

In long-distance running, there's a curious phenomenon known as the "marathoner's mile." Runners often hit a wall around mile 20, where fatigue feels insurmountable. But those who take a moment to celebrate small victories—like reaching the next water station—report feeling re-energized. The celebration doesn't have to be grand; even a mental cheer can reignite their resolve.

This lesson applies to our own lives. When the road ahead feels overwhelming, celebrating the smallest milestones can restore our strength to keep moving forward.

The Unexpected Power of Gratitude in Adversity

During the 2011 Tōhoku earthquake and tsunami, many communities in Japan were devastated. Yet, in the midst of despair, people found ways to honor what remained. Survivors gathered to express gratitude for their lives, their loved ones, and the support they received from others. These acts of gratitude and celebration didn't erase their pain, but they provided a vital source of hope and strength.

This story reminds us that celebration is about finding light in the darkness and using it as a beacon to move forward.

The Pitfall: Waiting for the "Perfect" Moment

One of the greatest barriers to celebration is the belief that it must wait for the "perfect" moment—the big promotion, the dream house, the ideal weight. But perfection is a moving target, and the danger of waiting is that we risk overlooking the moments that truly matter.

Think about the peach tree, whose blossoms are celebrated during *hanami* long before its fruit is ready. The Japanese understand that beauty exists in every stage of growth, from the first bud to the ripe harvest. We, too, can learn to find joy in our unfolding journey, without waiting for everything to be "just right".

Practical Lessons for Cultivating Celebration

Lesson 1: Celebrate the Small Wins

Start small. Did you take a single step toward a goal today? Did you show kindness to yourself or someone else? Every step counts.

- **Exercise:** At the end of each day, write down one thing you accomplished, no matter how minor it seems. Maybe you made your bed, completed a task at work, or took a walk. Say out loud, "I'm proud of myself for this", and let yourself feel the joy.

Lesson 2: Ritualize Your Progress

Create personal rituals to honor your milestones. These rituals don't have to be elaborate — they just need to be meaningful to you.

- **Exercise:** Choose a small, symbolic act to mark your achievements. For example, light a candle when you finish a challenging project, or treat yourself to your favorite tea after completing a week of consistent effort toward your goals.

Lesson 3: Share Your Joy

Celebration is amplified when shared. Invite others to honor your journey with you.

- **Exercise:** Once a week, gather with friends or loved ones to share one thing you're proud of. Create a space where everyone can celebrate their progress, no matter how small.

Lesson 4: Celebrate Even When You Stumble

Growth is rarely linear, and setbacks are a natural part of the process. Instead of criticizing yourself, celebrate the courage it took to try.

- **Exercise:** When you face a challenge or failure, write down one positive thing you learned from the experience. Acknowledge the effort you made, and thank yourself for showing up.

Cultural Celebrations of Progress

Different cultures have unique ways of honoring growth and milestones, offering valuable inspiration for our own celebrations.

- **Japan:** Beyond *hanami*, traditions like *shichi-go-san* (a festival celebrating children aged three, five, and seven) remind us to cherish stages of life that might otherwise be overlooked.
- **Mexico:** The *quinceañera* celebrates a girl's transition to womanhood, blending tradition with personal milestones.
- **India:** Festivals like *Diwali* emphasize the triumph of light over darkness, encouraging celebration even after challenges.

These practices show us that celebration can be woven into the fabric of life, making every step of the journey feel sacred.

Conclusion: The Joy is in the Journey

As you reflect on your own journey, consider this: How would your life change if you celebrated not just the destination, but every step along the way?

Celebration is an essential practice for flourishing. It reminds us that life is happening now, in every choice we make and every effort we put forth.

So light that candle. Raise that toast. Honor your path, no matter how winding or uncertain it may feel. Because every step forward is a testament to your courage, your resilience, and your commitment to grow.

Celebrate this moment, right here, as another step in your extraordinary journey.

VIII

Design Your Own Path

The Lonely Lantern on the Mountain Path

In the mountains of Nagano, there's a trail known for its breathtaking views and treacherous bends. Long ago, travelers braved the path under the light of a single lantern at the summit. Local legend tells of a craftsman who created that lantern—not to mimic the grand temples or bustling towns below, but to light the path for those who dared to climb.

When asked why he didn't copy the ornate designs of others, the craftsman replied, "This lantern doesn't guide crowds; it guides individuals. Its light bends with the wind, grows stronger in the dark, and will always shine where it is most needed".

The lantern is a powerful metaphor for our own lives. Too often, we attempt to follow paths laid by others, seeking to emulate their footsteps. But like that lantern, our true purpose is not to illuminate another's journey—it's to guide our own. Oubaitori reminds us that we were never meant to walk the same path as anyone else. Your life deserves its own design, its own rhythm, and its own light.

The Courage to Step Off the Beaten Path

From childhood, we are taught to look to others for direction—parents, teachers, mentors, society itself. While guidance is valuable, it can unintentionally narrow our vision, making us believe there is only one "right" way to live. Graduate from a prestigious school. Land a secure job. Start a family by a certain age. Yet, these paths are not universal—they're templates, not truths.

The Japanese concept of *jinsei no michi* (人生の道), or "one's own life path," teaches that every individual's journey is as unique as their fingerprint. Oubaitori aligns with this philosophy, urging us to embrace the idea that fulfillment comes not from following someone else's map but from drawing our own.

Yet stepping off the beaten path can be terrifying. Neuroscience reveals that humans are wired to seek comfort in the familiar. Following the herd feels safe because it reduces uncertainty. But while safety may protect us, it rarely fulfills us. The most meaningful lives are often forged in the wilderness of self-discovery, not on well-trodden roads.

Designing your own path requires two things: the willingness to question societal expectations and the courage to trust your inner compass.

The Wanderer Who Found the Way

Take the story of Naomi Uemura, a Japanese adventurer who became the first person to climb Denali (Mount McKinley) solo. His achievement was extraordinary, but what's even more remarkable is how he got there. Uemura didn't grow up in a family of mountaineers or study under famous explorers. Instead, he discovered his passion for the mountains by accident while living a quiet, unremarkable life in Tokyo.

His friends thought he was reckless. Experts doubted his abilities. But Uemura understood something many of us forget: the path to true fulfillment doesn't require anyone else's approval.

When asked why he took such risks, Uemura simply replied, "Because the mountains called me."

His story reminds us that the only map worth following is the one that leads to our own sense of purpose. What "mountain" is calling you?

Practical Lessons: Charting Your Unique Course

1. **Define Your North Star**

Ask yourself: What drives you? What makes you feel alive? These aren't questions to answer in haste—they require deep reflection.

- Spend time writing about moments when you felt truly fulfilled or joyful.
- Look for patterns: Is there a theme that emerges?
- Translate those themes into a clear, personal mission statement, such as:
    - "I want to create art that inspires empathy."
    - "I want to teach others how to heal through music."

This mission becomes your North Star, guiding your decisions and helping you filter out distractions.

2. **Break Free from the "Shoulds"**

Make a list of all the things you believe you "should" do—career paths, lifestyle choices, personal goals. Then, for each item, ask:

- "Is this truly mine, or is it an expectation placed on me?"
- "Does this align with my North Star?"
  Let go of the "shoulds" that no longer serve you.

3. Experiment Without Fear

Designing your own path doesn't mean you have to get it right the first time. In fact, failure is often the best teacher. Treat your life as an experiment:

- Try new hobbies, jobs, or ways of thinking.
- Reflect on what feels authentic and what doesn't.
- Adjust course without shame—growth isn't linear, and it's never too late to pivot.

4. Build a Supportive Environment

Surround yourself with people who respect your individuality. Share your vision with those who encourage you rather than judge you. Seek mentors who inspire but don't impose their paths on you.

5. Create Rituals That Ground You

Designing your path requires focus and consistency. Establish daily or weekly rituals that keep you aligned with your North Star:

- Morning affirmations: "I trust my journey."
- Weekly reflection: Write about how your actions this week brought you closer to your unique goals.
- Gratitude practice: Focus on the steps you've taken, no matter how small.

Conclusion: Light Your Lantern

Designing your own path isn't about rejecting others—it's about honoring yourself. Just as no two cherry trees bloom in the same pattern, no two lives are meant to follow the same trajectory.

You may feel doubt. You may encounter resistance. But remember this: every great journey begins with a single step, even if that step is onto untrodden ground. Trust that your inner light, like the lantern on the mountain, will illuminate the way.

As you walk forward, whisper to yourself:

- "I am the architect of my life."
- "I trust my instincts to guide me."
- "My path is valid, even if no one else understands it."

The world doesn't need another replica—it needs *you*. Design a life so authentic, so vibrant, that it becomes an inspiration for others to do the same.

And when you reach the summit of your own mountain, turn back to light the path for others. After all, the greatest journeys aren't just about reaching the destination—they're about becoming the person who dared to walk them.

IX

Flourishing in Community

The Garden That Grew Together

In a small village near Kyoto, there is a community garden known as "Kizuna no Niwa," or "The Garden of Connection." Unlike traditional gardens where individual plots are assigned to each family, this one thrives on collective effort. Neighbors plant together, tend to each other's crops, and share the harvest equally.

One year, a devastating storm swept through the area, flattening crops and washing away the soil. Many feared the garden would never recover. But the villagers refused to give up. Together, they rebuilt the beds, carried soil from nearby hills, and planted seeds again. That summer, the garden bloomed more vibrantly than ever before.

The garden became a living metaphor: while each plant grew on its own, its true strength came from the community that nurtured it. This is the essence of Oubaitori in community: flourishing not just as individuals, but as part of something larger, where each person's unique growth contributes to a shared beauty.

The Interconnected Nature of Growth

Oubaitori celebrates individual growth and the unique paths we all walk. Yet, even the most independent journeys are enriched by the connections we build with others.

In Japanese culture, there is a term called *wa* (和), which means harmony. While it often refers to societal balance, it also symbolizes the deep interdependence between individuals. A tree may grow tall and strong, but its roots intertwine with those of others, sharing nutrients and stabilizing the soil. Similarly, our growth is often supported by the unseen kindnesses of others: a friend who believes in us, a mentor who guides us, or even a stranger who inspires us.

Modern psychology supports this idea. Research from Harvard's longest-running study on happiness shows that strong relationships are the key to a fulfilling life. The quality of our connections—not our achievements or material success—most profoundly influences our well-being.

Yet, true connection requires vulnerability. In a world that often rewards self-sufficiency, asking for help or admitting our struggles can feel like weakness. But it is in these moments of openness that the richest relationships are forged.

Oubaitori reminds us that we do not grow in isolation. Just as cherry trees, plum trees, and peach trees can thrive in the same orchard, we flourish when we honor both our individuality and our shared humanity.

The Strength of the Mycelium Network

In the forests of Japan, beneath the surface of the soil, lies a hidden marvel: the mycelium network. This vast web of fungal threads connects tree roots across entire ecosystems, allowing them to share water, nutrients, and even warning signals about disease or pests. Scientists call it the "Wood Wide Web."

What's astonishing is how altruistic this network is. Older, stronger trees will send nutrients to weaker ones struggling to grow. Dying trees release their stored resources into the network, feeding the next generation.

This unseen network mirrors the power of human connection. When we act as a mycelium for each other—offering support, sharing wisdom, and lifting those who are struggling—we create an ecosystem where everyone can thrive.

The lesson is clear: the strongest communities are those that embrace generosity, empathy, and collaboration.

Practical Lessons: Building a Flourishing Community

1. Cultivate Genuine Relationships

- Focus on depth, not quantity. A few meaningful connections are far more nourishing than dozens of surface-level acquaintances.
- Be present: Put away distractions when spending time with loved ones. Truly listen, and offer your undivided attention.

2. Celebrate Diversity

Just as Oubaitori honors the unique rhythms of different trees, strong communities embrace differences in perspective, culture, and experience.

- Seek out people whose strengths complement

your own.
- Celebrate others' successes without comparison, knowing that their growth enriches the whole.

3. **Practice Mutual Support**

- Offer help without expecting anything in return. Acts of kindness often create ripples that return to you in unexpected ways.
- Don't hesitate to ask for help when you need it. Vulnerability builds trust and deepens connections.

4. **Engage in Collective Growth**

- Join groups or communities that align with your values, whether it's a book club, volunteer organization, or creative circle.
- Share your knowledge and skills generously, but also remain open to learning from others.

5. **Create Rituals of Togetherness**

- Host regular gatherings, even small ones, to connect with friends, family, or colleagues.
- Establish shared rituals, such as group gratitude practices or collaborative projects.

Conclusion: Blooming Together

In the heart of Oubaitori lies a profound truth: while your growth is unique, it is also deeply connected to the growth of others.

Imagine a garden where every plant thrives—not because it competes, but because it shares sunlight, water, and soil. This is the kind of community we should strive to build: one where each person's individuality is honored, yet everyone works together to nurture collective well-being.

As you reflect on your own path, consider how you can contribute to the flourishing of others:

- Is there someone who needs your encouragement?
- Can you offer a skill or resource to support someone's growth?
- How can you celebrate the diversity and beauty of those around you?

The most meaningful lives are not measured by personal achievements alone, but by the connections we nurture along the way. Together, we create a mosaic of growth, each piece unique, yet forming a breathtaking whole.

As you walk forward, remember the lesson of the mycelium: strength comes not from standing alone, but from growing together. Embrace your community as part of your journey, and you will find that your light shines brighter when it joins with others.

In the words of an old Japanese proverb:

"A single arrow is easily broken, but not ten in a bundle."

Let us flourish as individuals, yes—but let us also bloom as one.

X

The Impact of Blooming at Your Own Pace

The Ripple of a Single Bloom

In a quiet field outside Osaka, there is a lone sunflower that became a local legend. While most sunflowers grow and bloom in unison, this one lagged behind. The others flourished early in the summer, their golden faces turned toward the sun. By late August, they had withered, their petals scattered by the wind.

But as autumn approached, the lone sunflower began to bloom, defying the season. Passersby stopped in awe at its resilience, its golden petals glowing in the softer autumn light. It became a symbol for the town—proof that beauty doesn't adhere to a schedule, and that even a single bloom can light up the world.

This sunflower's impact didn't end in that field. Visitors carried its story home, inspiring others to embrace their own timing and share their light with the world.

Just like that sunflower, your choice to bloom at your own pace doesn't just transform your life; it creates ripples that touch others in ways you may never fully know. This chapter explores how embracing Oubaitori can influence not only your own growth but also inspire, heal, and uplift those around you.

The Power of Authentic Growth

When you embrace your unique journey, you create an authenticity that resonates far beyond yourself. Authenticity isn't just about being true to yourself — it's about showing up in the world as the person you were meant to be.

Psychologists call this phenomenon "emotional contagion." Just as laughter spreads in a crowded room, your confidence and contentment can influence the people you encounter. When you stop competing and start flourishing, you send an unspoken message: It's okay to grow at your own pace.

Consider the story of Masako Wakamiya, a Japanese woman who, at age 60, decided to learn programming. By 82, she had developed her own app, inspiring millions of seniors worldwide to embrace technology and challenge the narrative of aging. Her personal decision to grow late in life didn't just change her world — it reshaped perceptions of what's possible for others.

This is the quiet, transformative power of Oubaitori: your willingness to flourish authentically encourages others to do the same.

The Butterfly Effect of Personal Growth

In chaos theory, there's a concept called the "butterfly effect." It suggests that a butterfly flapping its wings in Brazil can set off a chain of events that ultimately leads to a hurricane halfway around the world.

This is a profound reminder that small actions have far-reaching consequences. In the same way, your personal growth, no matter how subtle, creates ripples that can transform the lives of others.

Take, for example, Nikola Tesla. In his time, Tesla's groundbreaking ideas, such as alternating current and wireless communication, were often ridiculed or overshadowed by competitors. Yet, Tesla remained steadfast, pursuing his vision with relentless dedication, even in the face of financial and personal hardship. Though he died in relative obscurity, today his innovations power the modern world, and his legacy is celebrated as one of the most brilliant inventors in history. Tesla's story exemplifies how staying true to your unique path, regardless of immediate recognition, can create a lasting impact that transcends time.

When you bloom at your own pace, you may not see the full extent of your impact. But rest assured, your growth sets things in motion that can inspire people far beyond your immediate circle.

Practical Lessons: Amplifying Your Positive Impact

1. **Share Your Story**

   - Speak openly about your journey, including your challenges and triumphs. Vulnerability is a powerful way to connect and inspire others.
   - Write, create, or speak in ways that reflect your truth. Whether it's a personal blog, a conversation with a friend, or a piece of art, your story has the power to touch lives.

2. **Model Compassion for Yourself and Others**

   - Show kindness to yourself when you

stumble—it teaches others that imperfection is part of the process.
- Celebrate the growth of those around you without comparison. Uplifting others only enriches your own journey.

3. **Plant Seeds of Encouragement**

- Offer words of support to someone struggling with their own growth. Sometimes, a simple "I believe in you" can spark transformation.
- Recognize the unique strengths of those in your community. Helping someone see their own potential is one of the greatest gifts you can give.

4. **Engage in Meaningful Acts of Service**

- Use your strengths to make a positive difference, whether it's mentoring, volunteering, or simply being present for someone in need.
- Remember: the greatest impact often comes from the smallest acts of kindness.

5. **Embrace the Long View**

- Understand that your growth doesn't need to result in immediate change. Trust that the ripples you create today may take years to reach their full effect.
- Stay patient and continue nurturing your own journey.

Conclusion: Becoming a Beacon of Authenticity

As you reflect on your journey through Oubaitori, consider the ways in which your growth has already touched others. Perhaps it was a moment of courage that inspired a friend to take a leap, or an act of resilience that showed someone the strength within themselves.

Your decision to bloom at your own pace is not just an act of self-love—it's a gift to the world. In choosing to honor your unique path, you remind others that they, too, can flourish in their own time.

Imagine a world where everyone embraces their individuality without fear of judgment, where growth is celebrated instead of compared. This is the ultimate impact of Oubaitori: it creates a culture of authenticity, where each person's light adds to the collective brilliance of humanity.

As the Japanese poet Ryōkan once wrote:

"The flower does not think of competing with the flower next to it. It just blooms."

By choosing to bloom authentically, you not only transform your own life—you inspire a cascade of courage, compassion, and creativity in others. Your journey matters, not just for yourself, but for the countless lives you'll touch along the way.

So step forward with confidence, knowing that your light, however small it may seem, has the power to illuminate the world. The ripples of your growth will reach further than you can imagine—just as the sunflower blooms not only for itself but for everyone who sees it.

XI

The Silent Forest – Finding Strength in Stillness

When the Forest Whispers

In the heart of Japan's Aokigahara Forest, also known as the Sea of Trees, an uncanny silence reigns. Walking through this dense forest, you hear no birdsong, no rustling leaves—only the muted sound of your own breath. For centuries, Aokigahara has been a place of introspection. Travelers, poets, and monks have ventured into its depths, seeking clarity in its quietude.

During one of my visits there, I met an elderly monk sitting beneath a towering cedar. I asked him why he chose this forest for his meditation. He replied with a faint smile, "The forest speaks. But to hear it, you must first quiet yourself."

His words stayed with me, revealing a powerful truth: growth often happens in stillness, in those moments when we pause and listen to our inner selves. In our world of constant noise—both external and internal—this silence has become rare, yet it is essential. Oubaitori teaches us that just as trees thrive in harmony within the forest, we too must embrace moments of stillness to grow deeply and authentically.

The Gift of Stillness

In modern society, we equate action with progress and noise with productivity. We are inundated with the need to *do more, achieve more,* and *be more.* But like a tree that grows quietly underground before its first shoot breaks the soil, true transformation begins in the unseen spaces.

Neuroscience offers a fascinating perspective: when the brain is at rest, it engages the "default mode network." This network, active during quiet reflection, plays a crucial role in creativity, problem-solving, and emotional regulation. Without moments of stillness, the brain's capacity to innovate and process deeply diminishes.

Culturally, however, we often fear stillness. Silence can feel uncomfortable, even threatening, because it forces us to face our own thoughts without distraction. Yet, just as the forest depends on its quiet rhythms — the sway of roots in the earth, the gentle hum of photosynthesis — our inner forest thrives on similar pauses.

The Power of Waiting to Bloom

In nature, some trees take years to bloom. The Chinese bamboo, for example, spends up to five years growing a complex root system underground before it shoots skyward. When it finally breaks the surface, it can grow up to 90 feet in just five weeks.

We, too, need time to build our roots. Stillness allows us to fortify ourselves for future challenges. It's not a lack of progress; it's preparation. History offers countless examples of individuals who thrived after periods of deliberate pause:

• During her lifetime, **Emily Dickinson** lived a reclusive life, sharing only a handful of her poems with the world. Her unconventional style and introspective themes were largely unrecognized and unappreciated in her era. Yet, after her death, the discovery of nearly 1,800 poems transformed her into one of the most celebrated figures in American literature. Dickinson's solitude and focus on her unique voice show how embracing one's individuality, even in isolation, can create a legacy that inspires generations.

- **J.K. Rowling**, before creating Harry Potter, spent years in financial hardship, using quiet reflection to craft her magical universe.

These periods weren't setbacks but essential stages in their journeys.

Surprising Lessons from Nature

The Underground Symphony

In forests, trees communicate through a hidden network of roots and fungi known as the mycorrhizal network, or "the wood-wide web." Through this network, older trees share nutrients and warnings with younger saplings. The process is slow and imperceptible, but it sustains the forest as a whole.

Similarly, our quiet moments often connect us to wisdom we didn't know we possessed. When we reflect, we tap into the deep reservoirs of our subconscious, gaining insights that aren't accessible in the rush of daily life.

The Cedar That Waited

In Yakushima, an island known for its ancient cedar trees, there's a particular cedar called *Jōmon Sugi*. Estimated to be over 2,000 years old, it's one of the oldest living organisms on Earth. Jōmon Sugi didn't become this resilient through constant growth; it thrived by enduring harsh winters, torrential rains, and long periods of dormancy.

Its patience reminds us that longevity and strength are born from enduring stillness, not from chasing constant motion.

Leaning into the Pause: Practical Lessons

Lesson 1: Create a Ritual of Stillness

Instead of waiting for life to force stillness upon you, carve out time for intentional quiet. This doesn't have to be meditation in a formal sense. It can be sitting on your porch at sunrise, savoring the first sip of tea, or simply breathing deeply in a moment of solitude.

- **Exercise:** Choose a recurring time each day — perhaps five minutes in the morning — to sit without distractions. Let thoughts come and go, like clouds drifting past a mountain.

Lesson 2: Trust Your Roots

When progress feels invisible, remind yourself of the bamboo. Growth often happens beneath the surface before it becomes visible. Instead of doubting your path, trust that the roots you're nurturing will sustain you when the time is right.

- **Exercise:** Write a list of ways you're investing in your personal growth that may not yet be visible. It could be learning a new skill, building relationships, or fostering emotional resilience.

Lesson 3: Detach from the Need for Constant Validation

Silence is a form of independence. When you embrace stillness, you step away from the need for external approval. This detachment allows you to focus on your own growth without distraction.

- **Exercise:** Challenge yourself to spend an afternoon offline, away from social media and notifications. Use that time to reconnect with yourself — through journaling, walking, or simply sitting in nature.

Conclusion: The Symphony Within

In the quiet of the forest, something magical happens. The absence of noise amplifies the subtler symphony of life: the rustling of leaves, the distant call of a bird, the quiet hum of the earth itself.

When we allow ourselves moments of stillness, we tap into this same symphony within. Our thoughts become clearer, our dreams more vivid, and our sense of purpose more profound. The monk in Aokigahara was right: the forest speaks, but only to those willing to listen.

So, pause. Find your own Sea of Trees. Not as a retreat, but as a space to nurture your roots, gather your strength, and prepare for your bloom.

When you emerge from this stillness, the world will see a version of you that is deeper, stronger, and more aligned with your true self. And when that happens, your journey won't just inspire you — it will inspire everyone who sees you thrive.

Let us now step forward into the next chapter, where we explore how to use the wisdom gained in stillness to cultivate resilience in the face of life's storms.

XII

Weathering the Storm – Cultivating Resilience Through Oubaitori

When the Wind Tests the Tree

In the mountains of Yakushima, where ancient cedar trees cling to rocky cliffs, storms rage with unrelenting force. The winds howl, the rain lashes, and yet the trees endure, their roots gripping the earth with unshakable strength. One might think these storms weaken the trees, but the opposite is true. The very act of withstanding such adversity makes them stronger.

Once, a local forester explained this phenomenon to me: "These trees are shaped by the storms. Without the wind, their roots would not reach so deeply, and their branches would not be so resilient."

Life is much the same. Challenges are inevitable, but how we face them determines whether we are uprooted or emerge stronger. Oubaitori offers a profound lesson here: just as no two trees face a storm in the same way, no two people endure hardship identically. Each person's resilience is forged in their own unique manner, shaped by their circumstances, strengths, and growth.

Resilience: The Art of Bending Without Breaking

What does it mean to be resilient? Popular culture often glorifies resilience as the ability to "bounce back," but that definition oversimplifies a complex process. Resilience isn't about returning to who you were before the storm. It's about growing stronger, deeper, and wiser because of it.

Research in psychology reveals that resilience isn't a fixed trait—it's a skill that can be cultivated. Studies by the American Psychological Association show that people who develop resilience share certain behaviors and mindsets:

1. **Adaptability:** The capacity to adjust to new circumstances without losing sight of long-term goals.
2. **Emotional Regulation:** The ability to manage stress and maintain focus during adversity.
3. **Support Networks:** Building relationships that provide strength and encouragement during difficult times.

These qualities align beautifully with the principles of Oubaitori. Instead of comparing ourselves to others' reactions or paths, we can focus on our unique way of weathering life's storms.

The Winds That Shape Us

The Storm of Self-Doubt

Everyone, at some point, feels the chilling gusts of self-doubt. It whispers that you're not enough, that others are doing better, or that you'll never overcome your current challenges. But here's the truth: self-doubt, like wind, is a natural force. It can push you down—or propel you forward, depending on how you harness it.

Take **Maya Angelou**, who, despite her remarkable achievements, admitted to feeling like an impostor throughout her life. Yet she used that doubt as fuel to write, speak, and inspire. Her storm didn't break her; it shaped her.

The Tempest of Failure

Failure often feels like a storm that uproots everything you've built. But consider the Japanese art of **kintsugi**, where broken pottery is repaired with gold, making the cracks part of the object's beauty. Resilience allows us to do the same with failure—integrating it into our story as a source of strength.

One striking example is **Thomas Edison**, who famously failed thousands of times before inventing the light bulb. When asked about his failures, he responded, "I have not failed. I've just found 10,000 ways that won't work." Edison's resilience turned his failures into stepping stones.

The Gale of Uncertainty

In a rapidly changing world, uncertainty can feel overwhelming. But trees don't resist the wind; they bend with it. Similarly, embracing uncertainty allows us to remain flexible and open to new opportunities.

A powerful case of embracing uncertainty comes from **Malala Yousafzai**, who faced unimaginable challenges in her fight for education. Instead of being paralyzed by fear, she used her uncertain circumstances to fuel her global advocacy.

Surprising Lessons from Nature and Culture

The Tree That Dances

In the Sahara Desert, there grows an unusual tree called the *Argan*. Its branches are so flexible that during sandstorms, it appears to "dance" with the wind rather than resist it. This ability to yield without breaking has allowed the Argan to thrive in one of the harshest environments on Earth.

Similarly, resilience isn't about standing rigid in the face of adversity; it's about learning when to bend and adapt.

The Japanese Metaphor of the Willow

In Japan, the willow tree symbolizes strength through flexibility. Unlike sturdier trees, the willow bends with the wind, avoiding the damage that more rigid trees sustain. This metaphor captures the essence of resilience: the ability to endure by flowing with life's challenges instead of resisting them.

Practical Lessons for Cultivating Resilience

Lesson 1: Anchor Yourself in Your Values

When the winds of adversity threaten to uproot you, your values act as an anchor. Knowing what truly matters to you provides stability.

- **Exercise:** Write down three core values that define who you are. During tough times, revisit these values to remind yourself of what grounds you.

Lesson 2: Build a Resilience Toolkit

Resilience is not just a mindset—it's a set of tools and strategies. Build your personal toolkit with practices that strengthen you emotionally, mentally, and physically.

- **Exercise:** Create a "Resilience Map." On a sheet of paper, draw three circles: one for people, one for habits, and one for beliefs. Fill each circle with resources you can lean on during challenges (e.g., supportive friends, meditation, your belief in perseverance).

Lesson 3: Reframe the Storm

Instead of viewing challenges as obstacles, see them as opportunities to grow. This mental shift can transform fear into motivation.

- **Exercise:** When facing adversity, ask yourself: "What is this storm teaching me? How can I use it to grow stronger?" Write your reflections and revisit them after the storm has passed.

Conclusion: Thriving in the Aftermath

Storms are inevitable, but they don't define us. What defines us is how we respond—whether we break, bend, or grow stronger. The ancient trees of Yakushima, the resilient willows of Japan, and the flexible Argan of the Sahara all teach us that resilience isn't about avoiding adversity but thriving because of it.

When the storm passes, the forest is often more vibrant than before. The rain nourishes the roots, and the wind clears away the dead branches.

You, too, can emerge from life's tempests renewed and stronger, with deeper roots and a clearer sense of purpose. Embrace the storms as part of your unique journey, and trust that every challenge is shaping you into a more resilient, authentic version of yourself.

As we move forward, the next chapter will explore how to celebrate your unique growth—not through comparison, but through the quiet confidence of knowing you're on your own extraordinary path.

XIII
Growing Through the Storm – Oubaitori in Times of Crisis

When the Ground Shakes

There's a Japanese saying: *Shikata ga nai* — "it cannot be helped." It reflects a quiet resilience in the face of adversity, a recognition that life's storms will come. But how we weather those storms defines the legacy we leave behind.

Imagine standing in a garden as a typhoon approaches. The trees bend and sway under the onslaught of wind and rain. Some lose branches, and others stand bare. Yet, when the storm passes, the roots that held firm grow stronger. This is Oubaitori in crisis — a way of embracing loss, uncertainty, or pain as seasons of transformation, not defeat.

In the moments when life feels fractured, when hope seems out of reach, the principles of Oubaitori guide us to stay grounded, honor our unique paths, and emerge not just intact, but renewed.

Finding Stability in the Chaos

In the face of a personal crisis — whether it's the loss of a loved one, a sudden change in circumstances, or a feeling of being unmoored — our first instinct is often to fight against it. Yet nature shows us another way: to pause, accept, and adapt.

Think of the plum tree during a late frost. Its blossoms might wither before they've had the chance to bloom. But the tree doesn't give up; it doesn't compare itself to the cherry tree that flowered early or the peach tree whose blooms came later. It simply focuses on survival, knowing another spring will come.

Your Path Through Crisis:

1. **Acknowledge the Storm:** Acceptance isn't surrender; it's recognizing the reality of the moment so you can respond to it with clarity. Write down what's within your control and what isn't—then focus your energy on the former.
2. **Anchor Yourself:** When everything feels uncertain, create small rituals that ground you. A cup of tea in the morning, a walk at sunset, or simply lighting a candle to remind yourself that even in darkness, light persists.

The Power of Perspective

When you're in crisis, it's easy to believe that your pain is unique, insurmountable. Yet Oubaitori teaches us to honor the diversity of life's experiences—not just the beautiful ones, but also the painful ones. Just as each tree endures its own challenges (drought, storms, disease), so too do we. But no tree grows without difficulty, and no life blossoms without moments of struggle.

Shift Your Inner Narrative:

- **Reframe the Pain:** Instead of asking, "Why

is this happening to me?" ask, "What can I learn from this?"

- **Seek Stories of Resilience:** Read or listen to stories of those who've faced similar storms and found their way through. Their journeys can offer hope and perspective.

Consider Viktor Frankl, a Holocaust survivor who, in the most unimaginable circumstances, discovered that even in suffering, meaning could be found. His story reminds us that while we cannot always control what happens to us, we can control how we respond.

Rebuilding After the Storm

Crises often strip us down to our core, revealing the foundations upon which our lives are built. This is an opportunity—a painful, yet profound one—to rebuild intentionally.

1. **Honor What Was Lost:** Grieve, cry, rage—whatever emotions surface, let them flow. Suppressing pain only deepens it.

2. **Redefine Your Values:** As you pick up the pieces, ask yourself: What truly matters? What do I want to carry forward, and what can I let go of?

3. **Set New Roots:** Begin small. If you've lost a job, focus on a skill you've always wanted to learn. If a relationship has ended, invest in self-discovery and friendships. Growth doesn't happen all at once; it happens in increments.

A Practice for Healing: The Kintsugi Journal

As we talked before, there is an art form in Japan called *kintsugi*, where broken pottery is repaired with gold, turning its cracks into something beautiful and unique. This practice mirrors the journey of healing—our scars, both visible and invisible, can become sources of strength and beauty.

The Kintsugi Journal Exercise:

1. Write down what feels "broken" in your life. Be honest and raw.
2. For each "crack," write what it has taught you or could teach you.
3. Imagine filling those cracks with gold—symbols of growth, resilience, and self-compassion.

For example:

"I lost my job, but it taught me the value of adaptability and showed me skills I hadn't realized I had."

Community as Shelter

When facing storms, remember that even the strongest trees thrive best in forests, their roots intertwined with others'. Seek connection during times of crisis—whether it's through friends, family, or support groups. Vulnerability isn't weakness; it's the courage to say, "I need help."

Conclusion: The Beauty of Renewal

Oubaitori reminds us that no season, no storm, lasts forever. Crisis may feel like the end, but it's often the beginning of something new—a reshaping of who we are, a deepening of our understanding, and a chance to bloom in ways we never imagined.

Just as spring follows winter, your time to blossom will come. Trust in your roots, honor your unique journey, and remember: even in the harshest storms, there is growth waiting to unfold.

Pause. Breathe. Write down one small act of care you can give yourself today—a reminder that you are growing, even now.

XIV

Cultivating Professional Success Through Oubaitori

The Untold Stories of Growth in the Workplace

In a bustling Tokyo office, four colleagues shared a similar start but diverged dramatically in their careers. While one climbed the corporate ladder swiftly, another took years to find their niche. A third ventured into entrepreneurship, and the fourth found fulfillment in a lateral move that aligned with their passions.

Each followed a different path, yet all eventually found success—on their own terms. The workplace often feels like an arena of competition, where faster, higher, and stronger seem to win the day. But in truth, professional growth, like personal growth, thrives when nurtured in alignment with our unique strengths and timing.

Oubaitori teaches us that in the professional and economic realms, success doesn't come from imitating others but from embracing your individuality. Just as each tree in a Japanese orchard blooms differently, each career path offers its own timing, lessons, and rewards.

In this chapter, we'll explore how the principles of Oubaitori can guide your professional journey, helping you design a fulfilling career while resisting the traps of comparison and burnout.

The Oubaitori Framework in the Workplace

The professional world often promotes a singular narrative of success: relentless ambition, immediate results, and measurable achievements. But this model overlooks the diversity of human growth and potential.

Oubaitori reframes professional success by focusing on four key principles:

1. Bloom in Your Season

Not everyone hits their stride at the same time. Early career achievers may shine brightly but burn out quickly, while late bloomers often thrive with longevity. Trusting your professional rhythm allows you to grow sustainably.

2. Nourish Your Roots

Behind every visible success lies an invisible foundation. Skills, relationships, and self-awareness are the roots that sustain long-term growth. Investing in these unseen elements ensures resilience when challenges arise.

3. Honor Your Unique Gifts

The workplace values specialization, yet individuality often gets sidelined. By leaning into your strengths and passions, you bring irreplaceable value to your role or industry.

4. Collaborate, Don't Compare

Viewing colleagues as collaborators rather than competitors fosters mutual growth. By supporting one another, you create a workplace culture where everyone can thrive.

Redefining Success

Consider the story of Sara Blakely, the founder of Spanx. Early in her career, she struggled to find direction, taking up various sales jobs before a moment of inspiration led her to invent a product that revolutionized the fashion industry. Her success didn't come from following a traditional corporate path but from trusting her instincts and pursuing an unconventional idea.

On the other hand, think of Ichiro Suzuki, the Japanese baseball legend. Ichiro's success wasn't built on raw talent alone but on disciplined, methodical growth. His ability to focus on incremental improvement over time made him one of the most consistent players in the sport's history.

Both stories illustrate that professional success is multifaceted. It's not about racing to the top but finding the intersection of your unique abilities, timing, and passion.

Practical Lessons: Applying Oubaitori to Your Career

1. **Discover Your Professional Rhythm**

   - Reflect on your career timeline. When have you felt the most engaged and fulfilled? Use those moments to identify your natural growth patterns.
   - Avoid rushing into promotions or career changes for external validation. Trust the timing of your journey.

2. **Build Invisible Assets**

   - Focus on skills that may not yield immediate

rewards but create long-term value, such as emotional intelligence, networking, or industry knowledge.
- Foster relationships based on trust and reciprocity rather than transactional exchanges.

3. Define Success on Your Terms

- Write down what success looks like for you. Is it financial security, creative freedom, meaningful impact, or work-life balance?
- Align your career goals with your personal values, not societal expectations.

4. Leverage Your Strengths

- Conduct a strengths assessment to identify your core competencies. Are you a visionary thinker, a detail-oriented planner, or an empathetic leader?
- Tailor your career path to roles that amplify your strengths rather than forcing yourself to conform.

5. Cultivate a Growth-Oriented Mindset

- Embrace setbacks as opportunities for learning rather than failures.
- Seek feedback not as criticism but as guidance for refinement.

6. Support the Growth of Others

Mentor a colleague, share insights, or celebrate someone else's achievements. A rising tide lifts all boats, and fostering growth in others often accelerates your own.

Conclusion: Becoming a Catalyst for Change

When you apply the principles of Oubaitori to your professional life, you transform not only yourself but also the environments in which you work. Your authenticity and confidence inspire colleagues, foster collaboration, and cultivate innovation.

Imagine a workplace where individuality is celebrated, where every employee feels empowered to bloom in their season. This is the kind of culture that Oubaitori promotes: one of shared success, mutual respect, and sustainable growth.

By honoring your unique journey, you set an example for others to do the same. You remind them that success isn't a race but a deeply personal exploration of potential. Together, we can redefine the professional world—not as a competitive arena but as a flourishing orchard where every individual contributes to the collective beauty of the whole.

As you move forward in your career, remember: your path is yours alone. Trust in your timing, embrace your strengths, and know that your authentic growth has the power to reshape not just your life but the lives of everyone around you.

The sunflower blooms at dawn, the moonflower at dusk. Both illuminate the world in their own way.

So, too, will you.

XV
Flourishing in Relationships Through Oubaitori

The Uniqueness of Every Bond

In a serene garden in Osaka, an elderly gardener tended to an assortment of plants, each one wildly different from the other. The roses were vibrant and fragrant, the ivy wove itself into the crevices of stone walls, and the succulents thrived in silence, needing only the occasional drop of water.

When asked why he didn't focus on cultivating just one kind of plant, the gardener replied with a smile, "Each has its own rhythm, its own needs. Together, they make the garden beautiful."

Relationships, like gardens, thrive not from uniformity but from understanding and honoring the uniqueness of each connection. Oubaitori reminds us that just as we must embrace our own individuality, we must also recognize and celebrate the individuality of those we love.

This chapter explores how the principles of Oubaitori can transform your personal relationships. By cultivating acceptance, patience, and authenticity, you can nurture bonds that are not only fulfilling but also deeply aligned with the beauty of mutual growth.

Oubaitori as a Framework for Relationships

Our modern world often pressures us to fit relationships into predefined molds. Whether it's the "ideal" romantic partnership, friendship, or family dynamic, we are bombarded with expectations about how connections should look and function.

Oubaitori offers an alternative: instead of striving for conformity, we honor the distinct rhythms and needs of each relationship. Just as the cherry, plum, peach, and apricot trees bloom in their own time, relationships flourish when we respect their natural flow.

Key principles include:

1. **Honor Individual Growth**

In healthy relationships, each person grows at their own pace. Recognizing and supporting this growth strengthens the bond rather than threatens it.

2. **Embrace Differences**

Differences in personality, communication styles, and goals aren't obstacles—they are opportunities to learn and grow together.

3. **Let Go of Comparison**

Comparing your relationships to others' can lead to resentment and dissatisfaction. Focus instead on the unique strengths of your connection.

4. **Cultivate Mutual Respect**

Relationships thrive when both parties feel seen, heard, and valued for who they truly are.

The Power of Diversity in Connection

Consider the story of Albert and Marie, a couple who couldn't have been more different. Albert loved solitude and books, while Marie thrived on social interactions and adventures. For years, they struggled to understand each other, often feeling as though they were speaking different languages.

One day, during a trip to the countryside, they visited a vineyard. The vintner explained how blending grapes from different varieties often produced the richest and most complex wines. Inspired, Albert and Marie began to view their differences as strengths rather than shortcomings. They learned to complement each other, and their relationship blossomed into a partnership of mutual admiration and growth.

Similarly, in friendships, colleagueships, and familial bonds, it's often the differences that bring depth and richness to the connection. Viewing relationships through the lens of Oubaitori allows us to appreciate diversity instead of fearing it.

Practical Lessons: Applying Oubaitori to Relationships

1. **Assess and Honor Each Relationship's Unique Needs**

- Ask yourself: What does this relationship need to thrive? Some bonds require regular communication, while others flourish with occasional check-ins.
- Adapt your approach to each person's preferences rather than imposing a one-size-fits-all model.

2. Practice Empathetic Listening

When engaging with someone, focus fully on their words, emotions, and unspoken cues. Empathy deepens understanding and connection.

3. Respect Boundaries

Just as trees grow best when they have space for their roots to spread, relationships thrive when boundaries are respected. Avoid overstepping emotional or physical limits.

4. Celebrate Milestones Together

Acknowledge and celebrate each other's achievements, no matter how small. Shared joy strengthens bonds.

5. Embrace Conflict as Growth

Disagreements are inevitable, but they don't have to be destructive. Approach conflicts as opportunities to learn about each other's needs and perspectives.

6. Let Go of Perfect Expectations

No relationship is without flaws. Perfection is not the goal; authenticity and mutual effort are.

Conclusion: A Symphony of Connections

Relationships, like a symphony, are composed of many different instruments playing in harmony. Each instrument has its own tone, rhythm, and role, yet together they create something greater than the sum of their parts.

When you approach relationships through the lens of Oubaitori, you create space for authenticity, mutual respect, and shared growth. You no longer see differences as divides but as bridges to deeper understanding.

Imagine a life filled with relationships where both you and your loved ones feel seen and celebrated for who you truly are. Such connections not only bring joy but also provide the strength to weather life's challenges.

As you nurture your relationships, remember the wisdom of the Osaka gardener: "Each has its own rhythm, its own needs. Together, they make the garden beautiful."

By cultivating relationships with care, patience, and the principles of Oubaitori, you create a personal ecosystem of love and support that mirrors the beauty of nature itself.

May your connections flourish, may your bonds deepen, and may you always find joy in the unique tapestry of relationships that enrich your life.

XVI

Cultivating Health Through Oubaitori

A Symphony of Balance

In the ancient practice of Shugendo, mountain monks in Japan developed a profound understanding of the human body as interconnected with the rhythms of nature. They believed that physical and mental health were not separate pursuits but two branches of the same tree. These monks didn't aim for peak performance or instant results; instead, they focused on harmony—listening to their bodies, respecting their limits, and nurturing their inner balance.

This philosophy aligns beautifully with Oubaitori. Just as cherry trees and plum trees thrive in different conditions, every person's path to health is unique. One may flourish with vigorous exercise, another with quiet meditation. One may heal through self-reflection, another through connection with others.

In this chapter, we will explore how the principles of Oubaitori can guide you to honor your unique health needs—both physical and mental. By rejecting comparison and embracing individuality, you can cultivate a lifestyle that supports long-term vitality and well-being.

Health Through the Lens of Oubaitori

The modern world often imposes rigid ideals of health—an "ideal" body shape, a perfect workout regimen, or a one-size-fits-all approach to mental well-being. These pressures not only create unnecessary stress but also distance us from understanding our true needs.

Oubaitori teaches us to view health as an individual journey rather than a competition. Just as each tree has its own season and way of flourishing, your health journey is shaped by your genetics, environment, experiences, and goals.

The Pillars of Oubaitori in Health

1. **Acceptance of Individual Rhythms**

Everyone's body and mind respond differently to challenges. Your energy, endurance, and mental resilience are uniquely yours. Recognizing this helps you set realistic expectations and avoid burnout.

2. **Honoring the Seasons of Life**

Your health needs change over time. What works in your 20s might not suit you in your 40s. Oubaitori encourages flexibility and adaptation to these transitions.

3. **Rejecting Comparison**

Comparing your fitness level, mental strength, or recovery speed to others' is counterproductive. Focus on incremental growth and celebrating small victories.

4. **The Interconnection of Body and Mind**

Physical health affects mental well-being, and vice versa. Adopting a holistic approach ensures that both aspects are nurtured together.

Stories of Transformation

The Marathon Runner and the Yogi

Consider the story of two friends, Aki and Reina. Aki was a marathon runner, pushing her body to its limits daily, while Reina was a yoga enthusiast, practicing slow, mindful movements. Aki envied Reina's calm demeanor and ability to manage stress, while Reina admired Aki's discipline and endurance.

After years of comparison, they decided to swap routines for a month. Aki discovered the power of stillness in yoga, feeling her body heal in ways she hadn't imagined. Reina, on the other hand, found joy in the exhilaration of running, building a strength she never thought she had.

Both realized that health isn't about choosing one approach over another — it's about listening to your body and finding what works for you at each stage of life.

Practical Lessons: Applying Oubaitori to Your Health

1. Listen to Your Body

Start each day by checking in with yourself. Are you feeling energized or fatigued? Adapt your activities to meet your current state rather than forcing yourself to follow a rigid plan.

2. Experiment Without Judgment

Try different forms of exercise, nutrition plans, or mental health practices. Whether it's weightlifting, swimming, mindfulness, or therapy, give yourself permission to explore what feels right.

3. Embrace Rest and Recovery

Like trees that take breaks between blooming seasons, your body needs time to recover. Overworking yourself — physically or mentally — can lead to long-term harm.

4. Mind Your Mindset

Practice self-compassion when you face setbacks. A missed workout or a difficult day doesn't define you. Focus on progress, not perfection.

5. Integrate Joyful Movement

Exercise shouldn't feel like punishment. Choose activities that bring you joy, whether it's dancing, hiking, or even gardening.

6. Nourish Your Body with Awareness

Rather than following the latest diet trends, pay attention to how different foods make you feel. A balanced diet is one that energizes and sustains you, not one dictated by societal pressures.

7. Prioritize Mental Health

Incorporate practices like journaling, meditation, or spending time in nature to support your emotional well-being. Seeking therapy or counseling when needed is a sign of strength, not weakness.

Conclusion: Your Unique Path to Health

Imagine a thriving forest. Some trees stretch tall into the sky, their leaves drinking sunlight. Others spread low and wide, their roots intertwining with those of their neighbors. Both are equally vital to the ecosystem, each contributing its own unique strengths.

Your health journey is no different. There is no single right way to thrive. By embracing the principles of Oubaitori, you can cultivate a lifestyle that respects your individuality, honors your natural rhythms, and supports both your body and mind.

As you walk this path, remember that health isn't a destination—it's a lifelong relationship with yourself. The small, daily acts of care you take for your body and mind ripple outward, enhancing every other aspect of your life.

When you honor your health with patience, acceptance, and joy, you not only flourish—you inspire others to do the same.

May your journey be filled with vitality, balance, and the quiet confidence that comes from living in harmony with yourself.

Epilogue

The Symphony of Your Own Bloom

As you close this book, I invite you to pause for a moment, place your hand on your heart, and feel the rhythm of life pulsing within you. This is your song, your tempo, your unique bloom unfolding. You have walked through these pages not as a passive reader but as an explorer, rediscovering the beauty of living in harmony with yourself and the world around you.

The concept of **Oubaitori** is not merely a philosophy—it is a way of being. It whispers to you that you are enough, just as you are, and that your path is as valuable as it is unique. It invites you to rise above comparison, embrace your individuality, and create a life that feels authentic to you.

A Journey Through the Seasons

We began by understanding the art of blooming at your own pace, learning from nature's wisdom that every tree, every flower, every life form has its moment to flourish. We then ventured into the quiet forest of inner dialogue, replacing harsh judgments with the gentle embrace of self-compassion. We explored the transformative power of gratitude, the joy of celebrating our uniqueness, and the strength found in honoring our journey rather than chasing destinations.

We delved into the professional world, the realm of relationships, and the intricate dance of health—applying Oubaitori's principles to every facet of life. Each chapter was a step forward, a deeper understanding of what it means to thrive in a way that is true to you.

The Power of Authentic Living

This book was never about giving you a map to follow—it was about helping you craft your own. You've been reminded that life is not a race but a garden where you are both the gardener and the bloom. The tools you've gained here are seeds: self-awareness, gratitude, individuality, resilience, and connection.

As you plant these seeds in the soil of your life, remember that growth takes time. Some blossoms will come quickly, and others will emerge after seasons of quiet care. Trust the process.

The Call to Action: Begin Today

Now is the time to take all you've learned and step into your own rhythm. What is one thing—just one—that you can do today to honor your unique path? Perhaps it's choosing kindness over self-criticism, finding gratitude in the small joys, or letting go of the need to compare your progress to someone else's. Whatever it is, begin. The smallest act, rooted in authenticity, can set profound change in motion.

Imagine a world where each person lived true to their nature. A world where we uplift rather than compete, where we see the beauty in our differences and celebrate the shared humanity that connects us all. You are a part of this vision. By embracing your individuality and blooming at your own pace, you inspire others to do the same.

A Final Reflection

Close your eyes for a moment and picture a forest. It's vast and diverse, filled with trees of every shape and size. Some stand tall and straight; others bend gracefully toward the light. Each one contributes to the harmony of the whole. You are one of those trees — unique, vital, irreplaceable.

Your journey does not end here; it begins anew. Carry Oubaitori in your heart as you step forward, not as a rigid rule but as a gentle reminder of your worth and potential. Trust yourself. Trust your seasons. Trust the bloom that is yet to come.

The world is waiting — not for perfection, but for you.

Go now, and flourish in the way only you can.

Final Chapter

Your Journey Begins – A Practical Guide to Embracing Oubaitori

A Map for Your Unique Path

You've explored the philosophy of Oubaitori, embraced its stories, and connected with its lessons. Now it's time to act. This chapter is your toolkit—a step-by-step guide to help you begin your journey of flourishing at your own pace. You don't need perfection or grand gestures; you just need willingness and small, consistent steps.

Let this be your mantra as you begin: *"Growth is not a race. It's a rhythm."*

Step 1: Reflect – Recognize Your Unique Rhythm

To begin, you must understand where you are and who you are. Reflection is the foundation of the Oubaitori journey.

Exercise: The Seasonal Audit

1. **Divide Your Life into Seasons:** Take a blank page and write these four categories: Spring (new beginnings), Summer (full bloom), Autumn (harvest and letting go), and Winter (rest and reflection).

2. **Assign Events to Each Season:** Reflect on your recent experiences and categorize them. For instance, a new job might belong in Spring, while a breakup could fit into Autumn.

3. **Identify Patterns:** What do you notice? Are you rushing to force Spring when you might need Winter's rest?

This exercise helps you embrace your current phase rather than comparing yourself to others in different seasons of life.

Step 2: Define – What Does "Blooming" Look Like for You?

Oubaitori is about flourishing in your own way, not by someone else's standards. To move forward, define your vision of growth.

Exercise: Craft Your Growth Statement

Answer these questions:

- *What does a fulfilled life look like to me?*
- *What are my core values?*
- *What gifts or strengths do I want to nurture?*

Write a statement that captures your unique aspirations. For example: *"My path to flourishing includes creativity, deep connections, and a life balanced between work and rest."*

Keep this statement visible as your compass.

Step 3: Act – Small Steps, Big Impact

Oubaitori doesn't demand dramatic life changes. Instead, it thrives on consistent, intentional actions.

Start with These Daily Practices:

1. **The Gratitude Anchor:** Begin or end each day by listing three things you're grateful for. This trains your mind to focus on abundance rather than scarcity.
2. **Micro-Growth Moments:** Dedicate 10 minutes a day to something that nurtures you—a hobby, learning, or quiet reflection.
3. **Nature as a Teacher:** Spend time observing nature's rhythms. A morning walk or even a glance out your window can remind you that growth is both subtle and powerful.

Step 4: Connect – Strengthen Your Roots

Your journey doesn't have to be solitary. Community plays a vital role in your growth.

Exercise: Build Your Support Forest

1. **Identify Your "Trees":** List people who inspire or support you—friends, mentors, or even authors and thinkers who resonate with you.

2. **Nurture Relationships:** Reach out to someone on your list this week, not to ask for anything, but to share gratitude or connection.

Strong roots in relationships help sustain you during life's storms.

Step 5: Reflect and Realign – Make it a Lifelong Practice

Growth is not linear; it's cyclical. Regular reflection helps you adapt and stay true to your unique path.

Monthly Check-In Exercise:

1. Review your Growth Statement: Is it still aligned with your values and desires?
2. Assess your Practices: Are your daily actions nurturing your growth? If not, what small shifts can you make?
3. Celebrate Progress: Reflect on how far you've come, no matter how small the steps may seem.

Tools to Support Your Journey

To help you stay on track, here are some practical resources:

- **Journaling:** Keep a dedicated Oubaitori journal for reflections, ideas, and milestones.
- **Mindfulness Apps:** Use apps like Headspace or Insight Timer to cultivate stillness and presence.
- **Inspirational Books and Stories:** Continue learning from others' journeys to deepen your understanding of Oubaitori.

A Final Word: Begin Today

The beauty of Oubaitori is that it doesn't demand perfection, nor does it compare your progress to anyone else's. Every step you take — no matter how small — is a step toward your own flourishing.

As you close this book, commit to one action. Whether it's writing your Growth Statement, taking a mindful walk, or reaching out to someone you care about, let today be the first step in your lifelong journey.

You are a cherry, a plum, a peach, or an apricot — and your season will come. Trust in your roots, nurture your branches, and watch your unique blossoms unfold.

www.ingramcontent.com/pod-product-compliance
Lightning Source LLC
LaVergne TN
LVHW041621070526
838199LV00052B/3204